SCHOLASTIC

writing guides

With interactive resources on CD-ROM

Scary Stories

for ages
7–9

Huw Thomas

C000108439

Credits

Author and Series Consultant
Huw Thomas

Development Editor
Simret Brar

Editors
Marion Archer and
Gaynor Spry

Assistant Editor
Sarah Sodhi

Series Designer
Anna Oliwa

Designer
Paul Stockmans

Cover Illustration
Mark Oliver

Illustrations
Sarah Warburton

CD-ROM Development
CD-ROM developed in
association with Infuze Ltd

Mixed Sources
Product group from well-managed
forests and other controlled sources
www.fsc.org Cert no. TT-COC-002769
© 1996 Forest Stewardship Council
FSC

Text © Huw Thomas
© 2009 Scholastic Ltd

Designed using Adobe InDesign

Published by Scholastic Ltd,
Villiers House,
Clarendon Avenue,
Leamington Spa,
Warwickshire
CV32 5PR

www.scholastic.co.uk

Printed by Bell & Bain

1 2 3 4 5 6 7 8 9   9 0 1 2 3 4 5 6 7 8

British Library Cataloguing-in-Publication Data
A catalogue record for this book is available from the British Library.

ISBN 978-1407-11267-1

Acknowledgments
The publishers would like to thank:
Johnson & Alcock Ltd for the use of an extract from *Black Jack* by Leon Garfield © 1981, Estate of Leon Garfield (1981, Longman Young Books).
Random House Group for the use of an extract from *The Wakening* by Paul Stewart © 1999, Paul Stewart (1999, Corgi).

CD-ROM Minimum specifications:

Windows 2000/XP/Vista		Mac OSX 10.4
Processor: 1 GHz	RAM: 512 MB	Graphics card: 32bit
Audio card: Yes	CD-ROM drive speed: 8x	Hard disk space: 200MB
Screen resolution: 800x600		

Contents

Introduction: Scary Stories

The *Writing Guides* series aims to inspire and motivate children as writers by using creative approaches. Each *Writing Guide* contains activities and photocopiable resources designed to develop children's understanding of a particular genre (for example, fairy stories). The activities are in line with the requirements of the National Curriculum and the recommendations in the *Primary Framework for Literacy*. The teacher resource books are accompanied by a CD-ROM containing a range of interactive activities and resources.

What's in the book?

The *Writing Guides* series provides a structured approach to developing children's writing. Each book is divided into four sections.

Section 1: Using good examples
Three text extracts are provided to explore the typical features of the genre.

Section 2: Developing writing
There are ten short, focussed writing tasks in this section. These are designed to develop children's ability to use the key features of the genre in their own writing. The teacher's notes explain the objective of each activity and provide guidance on delivery, including how to use the photocopiable pages and the materials on the CD-ROM.

Section 3: Writing
The three writing projects in this section require the children to produce an extended piece of writing using the key features of the genre.

Section 4: Review
This section consists of a 'Self review', 'Peer review' and 'Teacher review'. These can be used to evaluate how effectively the children have met the writing criteria for the genre.

What's on the CD-ROM?

The accompanying CD-ROM contains a range of motivating activities and resources. The activities can be used for independent work or can be used on an interactive whiteboard to enhance group teaching.
Each CD-ROM contains:

- three text extracts that illustrate the typical features of the genre
- interactive versions of selected photocopiable pages
- four photographs and an audio file to create imaginative contexts for writing
- a selection of writing templates and images which can be used to produce extended pieces of writing.

The interactive activities on the CD-ROM promote active learning and support a range of teaching approaches and learning styles. For example, drag and drop and sequencing activities will support kinaesthic learners.

Talk for writing

Each *Writing Guide* uses the principles of 'Talk for writing' to support children's writing development by providing opportunities for them to rehearse ideas orally in preparation for writing. 'Talk for writing' is promoted using a variety of teaching strategies including discussions, questioning and drama activities (such as, developing imaginative dialogue – see *Fantasy Stories for Ages 9–11*).

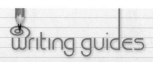

How to use the CD-ROM

Start screen: click on the 'Start' button to go to the main menu.

This section contains brief instructions on how to use the CD-ROM. For more detailed guidance, go to 'How to use the CD-ROM' on the start screen or click on the 'Help' button located in the top right-hand corner of the screen.

Installing the CD-ROM

Follow the instructions on the disk to install the CD-ROM onto your computer. Once the CD-ROM is installed, navigate to the program location and double click on the program icon to open it.

Main menu screen

Main menu

The main menu provides links to all of the writing activities and resources on the CD-ROM. Clicking on a button from the main menu will take you to a sub-menu that lists all of the activities and resources in that section. From here you have the option to 'Launch' the interactive activities, which may contain more than one screen, or print out the activities for pupils to complete by hand.

If you wish to return to a previous menu, click the 'Menu' button in the top right-hand corner of the screen; this acts as a 'back' button.

Screen tools

A range of simple writing tools that can be used in all of the writing activities are contained in the toolbar at the bottom of the screen.

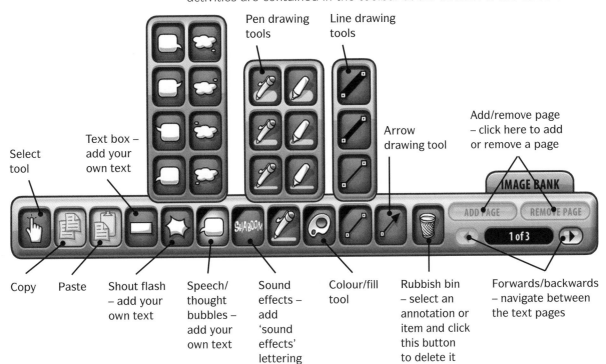

Pen drawing tools

Line drawing tools

Add/remove page – click here to add or remove a page

Text box – add your own text

Arrow drawing tool

Select tool

Copy   Paste   Shout flash – add your own text   Speech/ thought bubbles – add your own text   Sound effects – add 'sound effects' lettering   Colour/fill tool   Rubbish bin – select an annotation or item and click this button to delete it   Forwards/backwards – navigate between the text pages

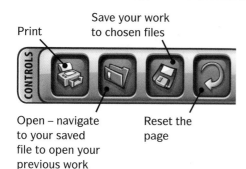

Print

Save your work to chosen files

Open – navigate to your saved file to open your previous work

Reset the page

Printing and saving work

All of the resources on the CD-ROM are printable. You can also save and retrieve any annotations made on the writing activities. Click on the 'Controls' tab on the right-hand side of the screen to access the 'Print', 'Open', 'Save' and 'Reset screen' buttons.

View all thumbnails by clicking on the arrows

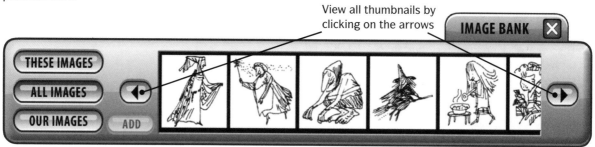

Image bank – click and drag an image to add it to an activity

Image bank

Each CD-ROM has an 'Image bank' containing images appropriate to the genre being taught. Click on the tab at the bottom right of the screen to open the 'Image bank'. On the left-hand side there are three large buttons.

- The 'These images' button will display only the images associated with the specific activity currently open.
- The 'All images' button will display all the photographs and illustrations available on the CD-ROM.
- The 'Our images' button will contain any images you or the children have added to the CD-ROM.

Press the left or right arrows to scroll through the images available. Select an image and drag and drop it into the desired location on the screen. If necessary, resize the image using the arrow icon that appears at the bottom right of the image.

You can upload images to the 'Image bank', including digital photographs or images drawn and scanned into the computer. Click on 'Our images' and then 'Add' to navigate to where the image is stored. A thumbnail picture will be added to the gallery.

Writing your own story

Each CD-ROM contains a selection of blank writing templates. The fiction genre templates will be categorised under the button 'My story' and the non-fiction templates will be categorised under 'My recount' or 'My writing'. The writing templates encourage the children to produce an extended piece of genre writing. They can also add images, speech bubbles and use other tools to enhance their work.

The fiction titles also include a cover template for the children to use. They can customise their cover by adding their own title, blurb and images.

Section 1
Using good examples

Scary story features

Structure
- Setting generates atmosphere and builds tension
- An 'It' factor – something out there to be feared
- Building up of suspense, keeping the reader waiting for a discovery
- A mystery that the reader wants to solve
- A back story – something in the past that leads to the mystery characters now encounter
- Characters survive, against the odds
- Clues point towards the solution to a mystery.

Language features
- Paragraphs that draw the reader into the atmosphere
- Main participants are vulnerable and caught up in a scary situation
- Atmospheric verbs – characters 'creep' and doors 'creak'
- Descriptive words create the atmosphere
- Adjectives that describe how the characters feel about what they encounter.

Using scary stories

Scary stories play with the feelings of their readers. The reader's response is manipulated by the way in which the tale plays upon our deepest fears. Such writing needs to be presented in a clever way: not being too obvious, but using techniques such as suspense and setting an atmospheric scene to draw the reader into the mood of the story. All writing is produced with some awareness of the audience who will read the text. In scary writing, this awareness is focused on two features: what ideas the reader will find scary, and how they can be gradually filtered through to the reader.

Getting to know the genre

The extracts featured in this section demonstrate good examples of scary writing, with features that children can adapt for their own work. Stress to the children that, as they read these texts, they are reading as scary writers. This means they should not only read the texts for enjoyment, but also look for features that make texts scary and then apply similar techniques to their own writing.

The extracts show how vocabulary is selected and how settings are described in order to create an atmosphere, while the actions of characters are presented in a way that gradually heightens the sense of fear and suspense.

Scary stories and the Primary Framework

To develop their own enthusiasm for, and skill of, scary writing children need to be exposed to good examples and it's worth spending some time reflecting on how they worked. How did they grab the reader and make them shiver?

'The Wakening' and 'The Eyes' extracts both go to the heart of good scary writing – characters in a frightening situation, causing the reader to feel what they feel. In the first example these feelings are prompted by a characters route through the setting, in the second and encounter with a character. Both employ a degree of suspense to slowly affect the reader, raising questions for them to seek the answers to. Both draw us into the experience of a central character, asking ourselves how we would have felt in that situation. In fact, if we can use scary texts as a means of teaching children how to enter the experience of another and write from that alternative point of view, we've scored a massive hit in our nurturing of young writers.

Extract 1: 'The Wakening'

What's on the CD-ROM

The Wakening
- Text extract to read and discuss.

Enter the clearing
- Drag and drop steps from the story into the correct order.

This extract illustrates how scary stories build suspense for the reader.

- Open the CD-ROM file 'The Wakening' and read the extract to the children. As you read this extract highlight the gradual way suspense is built up.

- Either on screen or using photocopiable page 10 'The Wakening', ask the children to number the steps and stages between Sam entering the clearing and the 'BANG' of surprise. These paragraphs are short, so number them and ask: *What happens in each one to build atmosphere?* Note the way Sam's senses play such a vital part in this process – he hears, he speaks and he sees. Circle the different senses in the text.

- Open the CD-ROM file 'Enter the clearing'. In this activity the children explore the suspense-filled build up to Tom seeing the shape in the clearing. Make sure the children don't have access to the original text extract. Then encourage them to place the steps in the story into the correct order by dragging them to the appropriate boxes. There are features in the text, such as an obvious opening line and the way Sam's sight gradually evolves, that will give them clues to the order. Emphasise to the class the way Sam's perception is gradually developed through the text.

- Alternatively, ask them to complete photocopiable page 13.

Extract 2: 'Black Jack'

What's on the CD-ROM

Black Jack
- Text extract to read and discuss

Dorking's feelings
- Drag and drop thought bubbles into the correct order.

This extract can be used to help the children focus on the way in which an event can be expanded with different emotions and details to develop the atmosphere and grab the reader's attention.

- Write on the board: 'Dorking sat in the room for two hours, then Black Jack's eyes opened.' Then open the CD-ROM file 'Black Jack' and as you read the extract, compare it with that single sentence.

- As a class list what happens while Dorking sits in the room. Look for words that show what he was thinking and feeling. Focus on the effect of the words 'In the eyes?' and the turning point this represents in the passage.

- Open the CD-ROM file 'Dorking's feelings' and hand out copies of photocopiable page 14. Ask pairs to read and order Dorking's thoughts, as they occur in the extract. Then ask the whole class to sequence these feelings on screen. Encourage them to refer back to the original text to see if they can recall what prompted each feeling.

- Hand out copies of photocopiable page 15 'Scare and compare'. Encourage the children to refer back to the original texts as they work to compare extracts 1 and 2.

Extract 3: 'The Whisperers'

This extract plays upon the reader's fear of the unknown. Two characters are in a spooky cottage, at night, and alone.

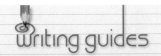

What's on the CD-ROM

The Whisperers
- Editable text extract to read and discuss.

Question time
- Read and discuss questions raised by the extract.
- Type a list of five more questions raised by the extract.
- Select five questions and answer them in order to develop the story further.

- Start by opening the CD-ROM file 'The Whisperers' and reading through the passage. Invite the children to tell you what they learn about the characters from reading the text. The reader is told how many there are in the cottage, but no names are provided. Ask: *What effect does this have on us as readers?*

- Open the CD-ROM file 'Question time' (or hand out copies of photocopiable page 16) and look through a selection of questions that are raised by this particular passage. Ask the children if they can think of any others. Make a list of the five biggest questions that spring from the text. Which ones would the children most like to see answered? Which ones do they think will be answered as part of the story? Are there any that don't really matter?

- Story telling is about narrowing possibilities. Look at four possibilities and ask the children what they think is most likely: Dad may or may not be safe; the scream in the night may or may not be the same voice as one of the whisperers; the whisperers may or may not be dangerous; the knock on the door may or may not be dad.

- Ask the children to work in groups of five and using the CD-ROM file 'Question time' (or photocopiable page 16) select five questions that they most want to discuss. Working in their groups can they come up with answers that will take the story to its next stage? One rule – dad, brother and sister must all survive in some form or other!

Poster: Scary writing

What's on the CD-ROM

Scary writing
- Read and discuss the poster information.
- Roll over each point to display examples from *The Wakening* extract.

- Open and display the CD-ROM poster 'Scary writing' (or enlarged photocopiable page 18 'Scary writing' to A3 poster size) and explain to the children that it refers back to some of the stylistic features they have encountered in this section.

- The poster can be used for shared activities and as a prompt for scary writing, as it encourages the children to identify techniques they have encountered in their reading and to apply these techniques to their own writing. It also aids evaluation as the points on the poster can be used as a checklist for their stories.

- As a class read through the CD-ROM poster and for each of the four points ask the children to provide examples of how these techniques have been used in the three extracts. Hand out copies of photocopiable page 17 'Scary scenes' for the children to record their examples from the three extracts.

- After discussing the children's ideas, roll over the four poster points to reveal examples of how these techniques are deployed in the extract from *The Wakening*.

Extract 1: The Wakening

'How much further?' he complained.

As if in response, the trees seemed to part and, as Sam stepped forward, he found himself in the circular clearing once again. With his heart racing and his stomach churning, he peered into the gloom.

All around him, he heard the sound of sharp intakes of breath. Sam stopped.

'It's too dangerous,' he whispered to himself. 'If only I could see.'

No sooner had the words left his mouth, than Sam found he could see – and instantly wished he could not. It all happened so fast.

As the fog thinned, Sam saw a dark shape in front of him; a shape which – as the fog dissolved completely – revealed itself as a small, hunched creature in dirty rags. It was standing with its back to him.

Sam stared in horror at the lowered head, terrified that the creature would look round. Scarcely daring to breathe, he began to back away. He hadn't gone more than two steps when he heard a sudden BANG! Echoing around the forest. The creature raised its head.

by Paul Stewart

Illustrations © 2009, Sarah Warburton.

Extract 2: Black Jack

Was he to be held in this dark, smelly and fearful room till ten? His master's shop was locked at seven: the family went to bed at nine...

He banged on the door and shouted 'Help!' five or six times. No one answered: no one came – and his own voice seemed to linger unsuitably in the air. He looked to the coffin, now shrouded in darkness. Had he – had he waked the enormous dead?

Against the faint window he saw Black Jack's feet. They were rooted still in the same patch of air – standing, so to speak, half-way up the window pane... He returned once more to his chair and rested his head against the fireplace wall.

Though he desired strongly to sleep out the hours remaining, sleep would not come. The presence in the coffin seemed to hold it at bay... as if the great death shamed the little one and would not let it come.

Now, little by little, the moon climbed out of the invisible chimney pots, turning the window to dull silver, so that it hung in the dark wall like an old tarnished mirror, capable of nothing but spite.

With a sigh of relief Dorking heard a clock strike nine. His vigil was almost done. He stood up and began to walk softly about the room – to ease the cramp in his legs and ward off the night's chill.

The silver moonlight, very bright now, seemed to lend the dingy room an odd beauty – as if it was intricately fashioned out of shining grey lead. Even the coffin and the still ruffian within it seemed carved and moulded by a master hand.

How finely done was the tangled hair – the knotted brow – the powerful, thick nose... how lifelike were the deep grey lips. How – how miraculously shone the moon in the profound eyes –

In the eyes? In the *eyes*? Sure to God those eyes had been shut before?

Those eyes! They were open wide! They were moving! They were staring at him!

by Leon Garfield

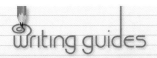

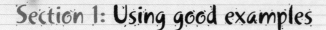
Extract 3: The Whisperers

'Come away from the window,' my brother said. He knew what I was looking for. He had heard the stories.

'Dad's been gone so long!' As I said it I felt my mistake sending me cold. When you're in the spookiest cottage in a woods in darkest Buckinghamshire, you don't say things like that. If you say things like that you start everyone thinking. And there was a lot to think about. We both remembered last night. We remember waking in the night and hearing the noise outside, the sound of a grown man screaming loudly, then stopping.

'What was it?' I had shouted out.

'Quiet' my dad had whispered sharply.

It felt like we sat there all night, waiting, listening, wanting it and not wanting it to come again. Eventually my brother said,

'What was it?'

What does my dad do? Suddenly he turns back into Mr Isn't-this-fun. Suddenly he just brushes the fears away with,

'Probably a fox. They do that, you know.'

That was not a fox. That was something out there, something that vented it's rage and grief in one long howl. It was out there, and dad, who had just gone to use the phone at the neighbour's farmhouse, was out there too.

'Come away!' my brother said again, this time insistent. His voice was trembling. He may be ten years older, but I heard him sound small. So I drew the curtains and sat beside the fire, and that's when it began. The whispering. Back there at the very window I had just left, a voice, whispering. It was as if the hushed tone seeped through the gaps in the pane, and what started as a shuffle of hush became words:

'This is not your home! This is not your home!'

One voice, then another. A man, a woman, a child.

'This is not your home!'

My brother stared at me. Neither of us could say a word, and then... the door thundered with a banging that shook the room.

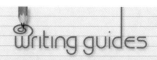

Enter the clearing

- The boxes below contain Sam's steps into the nightmare clearing. Without reading the text can you put these in the order in which they occurred?

...as Sam stepped forward, he found himself in the clearing once again.

With his heart racing and stomach churning, he peered into the gloom.

Sam found he could see – and instantly wished he could not.

Sam saw a dark shape in front of him;

'It's too dangerous,' he whispered to himself. 'If only I could see.'

All around him, he heard the sound of sharp intakes of breath. Sam stopped.

Section 1: Using good examples

Dorking's feelings

- The thought bubbles contain five things that Dorking felt during his time in the room with Black Jack's coffin.
- Discuss with a partner why he had each feeling. Stick them on paper in the order in which he felt them.

I thought something was beautiful. It was...

I strongly desired...

I felt relief because...

I felt sure that...

I felt full of fear when...

I felt it was miraculous how...

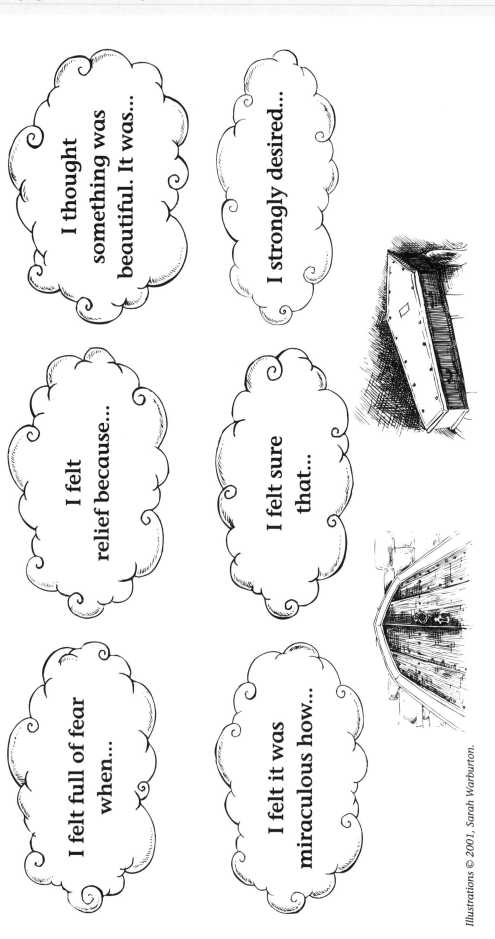

Illustrations © 2001, Sarah Warburton.

writing guides

Scare and compare

● Look at the extracts from *The Wakening* and *Black Jack*. Find the words used to tell the reader about the scary situations in each passage.

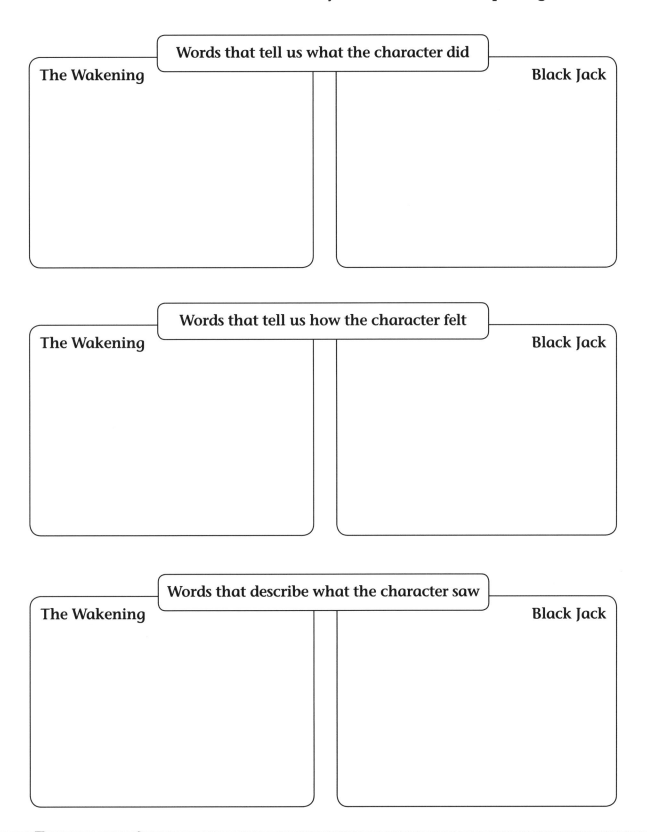

Words that tell us what the character did	
The Wakening	Black Jack

Words that tell us how the character felt	
The Wakening	Black Jack

Words that describe what the character saw	
The Wakening	Black Jack

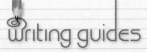

Section 1: Using good examples

Question time

● Read and discuss the eight questions below which are raised by
reading *The Whisperers*.

What is she looking for?	Why did dad go to the phone?
What are the stories?	Who are the Whisperers?
Was it a man's scream and why did he do this?	Why are the Whisperers saying that?
Was it a fox making that noise?	Who is at the door?

● Now make a list of five more questions raised by the extract.

1. _____

_____

2. _____

_____

3. _____

_____

4. _____

_____

5. _____

● Select five questions from either list, discuss them and then create
answers for each that will develop the story to the next stage.

Scary scenes

● In the table below record examples of how the four techniques have been deployed in each of the three extracts.

	The Wakening	Black Jack	The Whisperers
Reader questions			
Suspense moments			
Frightening and tense setting			
Characters' feelings			

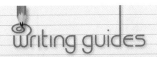

Scary writing

The reader has lots of questions.

The reader is kept in suspense.

The setting is frightening and tense.

The character's feelings are described.

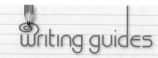

writing guides

Section 2
Developing writing

Capturing ideas

Scary writing provides an opportunity for children to enthuse in the slash and gore they love. Of course, many scary films are not accessible to children but a film like *The Wizard of Oz* contains important features.

Setting and back story

The scary place is constructed by having somewhere that is either evidently frightening, like a spooky house, or somewhere like a family home that becomes spooky when gremlins enter. Either way, scary writers should think of a back story. What mystery has led to this scenario?

Clues

Throughout the story clues should be scattered that can help characters figure out what is going on, why this scary situation exists and, when the confrontation happens, how to win. Harry Potter stories tend to hide the secret to winning earlier in the book.

Characters

Once the scary situation has been established characters need to be drawn there. If it's a normal setting gone bad they may already be there – many urban myths start during car journeys or babysitting. However, characters can end up in haunted houses because they are lost, dared or on a mission.

Suspense

Suspense is a critical feature so authors need to keep readers aware something wicked is coming – but it has to take some time to appear to build the atmosphere. The children will be writing in a way that lets readers sense the fearsome place, which will include thinking about the feelings and senses of characters during each part of the story.

Confrontation

The confrontation is a massive climax as that final encounter is where all is revealed. The ghouls are unmasked and characters face their fear. Somehow, unless everyone is to die, the characters need to be saved. To do this, the children need to learn the twin strategies of escape and defeat. Remember how Dorothy defeated the witch in *The Wizard of Oz*? There must be a way of finishing off the fear.

Activity 1: Are you getting scared?

Objective

To identify features that writers use to provoke readers' reactions (Year 3 Strand 8).

What's on the CD-ROM

Are you getting scared?
- Type in a typical fear and responses that explain reasons for this fear.

What to do

Scary writing preys upon fears so we can start by exploring our own.

- Open the CD-ROM file 'Are you getting scared?' and ask the children to name a typical fear. Stress that the fear could be either their own or someone elses, such as a fear of height or spiders.

- Write the most popular fear in the empty box in the centre and ask individuals to suggest descriptive words or reasons for the fear, writing these around it. For example, 'heights' may prompt the word 'falling'.

- Once this process is clear, arrange the children into groups of five and provide copies of photocopiable page 25 'Are you getting scared?'. Explain that they are going to map out five different fears. The children in each group should take turns to name and write a fear in an empty circles, while the rest write words and reasons around it.

- This activity will help the children create responses to fears that can be built up around a central scary idea. Possible ideas may include 'big dogs', 'dark cellars' and 'spooky woods'.

- Display this work as the feelings and descriptions evoked in this activity will be useful when considering characters' feelings in scary situations.

Activity 2: Feature feelings

Objective

To use settings and characterisation to engage readers' interest (Year 4 Strand 9).

What's on the CD-ROM

Media resources
- Use the 'Wooden chest' photograph as a stimulus for writing.

Feature feelings
- Drag and drop images of mysterious features to questions they may raise.

What to do

Moving on from a general exploration of fear as an emotion this activity explores how it works in the context of a mystery story.

- Display the image of the 'Wooden chest' from the 'Media resources' section of the CD-ROM. (Alternatively, show a sealed envelope or locked cash box – the more mysterious the better.) Explain that this object is locked inside a glass-doored cupboard in a typical mystery story. Then ask them to use their imagination and tell you what a character might think or feel as they look at the object. Their responses may include questions, hunches about what the object might contain or feelings evoked by it. Pick out these three strands within their responses.

- Provide the children with copies of photocopiable page 26 'Feature feelings' and ask them to record overleaf what a character may think or feel when seeing each of the mysterious features. Refer to the three types of thought and feeling.

- Open the CD-ROM file 'Feature feelings' which contains a list of eight possible questions that may arise when looking at the four mysterious features. Ask the children to match each of the eight questions to one or two of the four mysterious features located in the 'These images' section of the 'Image bank'. Note that some of the questions, such as 'Should I open it?' draw children further into the feelings surrounding the stimuli.

Activity 3: Feature feelings paragraph

Objective

To identify features that writers use to provoke readers' reactions (Year 3 Strand 8).

What to do

Continuing the work on 'Feature feelings' this activity focuses on writing.

- Organise the children into groups of four, sharing responses they had to the scary settings on photocopiable page 26 'Feature feelings'.

- Ask the children to select one of the features and decide which response is the most interesting for this feature and expand their original thoughts, using photocopiable page 27. Then invite each group to plan a paragraph that starts with the character seeing their chosen feature. They should start with 'Just then I saw a...' and go on to include the questions, hunches and feelings developed in their planning.

- Point out that characters in scary stories often seem rather naïve. Whereas most people in a creaky old house would run if they heard a noise in the attic, many characters go up the stairs. When reading a scary story like this, we may think 'Don't go up the stairs!' Can the children tease the reader in this way as the character contemplates what to do? Can they manipulate the reader to want to shout a warning?

- Ask a scribe to write up their group's paragraph and then invite them to individually devise a short story involving their chosen feature.

Activity 4: Scary places!

Objective

To use settings and characterisation to engage readers' interest (Year 4 Strand 9).

What's on the CD-ROM

Scary places!
- Select four cards to form the basis of a scary setting.
- Type a descriptive paragraph which creates a scary setting.

Media resources
- Use the 'Spooky house' image to stimulate ideas about setting.
- Play the 'Eerie wind' audio clip to stimulate ideas about setting.

What to do

In this activity the children will consider what makes a scary setting.

- Begin by asking the children to think of a good setting for a scary story. Insist they do not choose a haunted house but examples could include a derelict factory or a boarding school.

- Open the CD-ROM file 'Scary places!' and click on one card from each category (location, time of day, weather and sounds). Then as a class use the four selected cards to write a descriptive paragraph of a scary setting.

- Allow time for the children to select their own four cards and use them to independently plan and write a descriptive paragraph on photocopiable page 28 'Scary places!'. You also have the option to display the 'Spooky house' image and play the 'Eerie wind' audio clip, both from the 'Media resources' section of the CD-ROM, and let the children incorporate them into their own paragraph about a setting.

- Alternatively, they could use their initial idea for a setting and think up at least four new features not on the cards to make their setting as scary as possible. Their features could include details of the place (such as cobwebs or mice scuttling by) or words (such as 'eerie' or 'isolated') that will enhance the description.

- Whichever option chosen, encourage the children to include as much detail as they can about the setting.

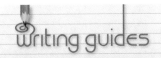

Activity 5: Suspense planner

Objective

To show imagination through the language used to create emphasis, atmosphere or suspense (Year 4 Strand 9).

What to do

Scary stories raise questions and give answers. In between they keep the reader in suspense.

- Ask the children what suspense is (when the reader is kept waiting for an event to happen or a question to be answered). Why do they think suspense is a good thing in scary stories? (It keeps the reader in a state of tension, imagining what might happen.)

- Hand out photocopiable page 29 and ask the children to think of a question that a scary story might raise, answer it and then write their question and answer in the boxes marked 'question' and 'answer'.

- Explain that in a scary story, the characters do not usually gain immediate answers to their questions. There are gaps, during which the reader is kept in suspense. The reader's imagination supplies all kinds of scary answers. Examine the example shown at the top of photocopiable page 29. Note that in the example the character is distracted by sounds outside. 'Just then, I thought I heard footsteps outside. Someone was coming. Who was it? Possibly the maid.'

- Ask the children to think of two things that can cause a delay in finding the answer and then to write each in the boxes between the completed question and answer boxes.

Activity 6: Reading questions

Objective

To identify features that writers use to provoke readers' reactons (Year 3 Strand 8).

What's on the CD-ROM

Media resources
- Use the image of the 'Open door' as a stimulus for writing.

Reading questions
- Select and type in story events and the questions they will raise in the reader's mind.

What to do

This activity helps children plan key parts of a scary or mysterious story.

- Reviewing responses to the extracts in Section 1, remind the children of the way in which scary stories raise questions in the reader's mind. Explain that they need to take parts of the story they are planning and think of questions the reader might ask while reading these parts.

- Model this process by displaying the image of the 'Open door' from the 'Media resources' section of the CD-ROM. Then ask: *As a reader what questions would be raised in your mind if you encountered this?*

- Open the CD-ROM file 'Reading questions' and first agree on a scenario in which a character would encounter this open door. Then type in the reader questions the children think this feature would raise.

- Ask the children to plan their own questioning moments either onscreen or using photocopiable page 30. Remind them to focus on features that trigger questions by presenting a mysterious new twist.

- Another way of approaching this task is to plan new sections of a story that are designed to prompt questions. For example, a character who is later to see smugglers on a beach might initially see a light out at sea, leaving the reader to ask: 'Who is shining the light?'

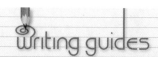

Activity 7: Bin bag clues

Objective

To offer reasons and evidence for their views, considering alternative options (Year 4 Strand 1).

What to do

Mystery stories need clues that point towards the solution to the puzzle.

- Arrange the class into small groups of four or five and provide them with a bin bag containing 'clues' around which a scenario can be constructed (photocopiable page 31 contains illustrations suitable for use as clues). For example, a bus ticket, a yoghurt pot, a message (such as 'Town Hall at 6.10').

- Tell the groups that it is the rubbish left by someone who has mysteriously vanished (or been abducted).

- Using five of the clues picked out a random, they should try piecing together the last movements of this person to build up a story. For example, the missing person ate a yoghurt, drank orange juice, took a bus to the town hall and met someone.

- This activity can be directed in various ways by providing a variety of 'clues', such as intriguing postcards, letters, newspaper advertisements, photographs or maps. Bear in mind that while you may be presenting these 'clues' with a particular narrative in mind, the children may reach a very different interpretation – encourage imagination as well as logic!

Activity 8: Clues

Objective

To use beginning, middle and end to write narratives in which events are sequenced logically and conflicts resolved (Year 3 Strand 9).

What's on the CD-ROM

Clues
- Type in the solution to a mystery and then click the 'Hide' button to conceal it.
- Create and type in clues that will help characters and readers solve the mystery.
- Click 'Reveal' to uncover the solution to the mystery.

What to do

This activity works backwards from the moment of revelation to the way in which clues can be scattered throughout the story.

- Discuss the way in which clues can be pieced together to solve a mystery, referring to examples from TV detective series.

- Open the CD-ROM file 'Clues'. Help the children devise a mystery, like a stolen necklace being taken by a trained assassin. Type this into the CD-ROM screen and then click on the 'Hide' button to model the fact that while the clues appear in a story, the denouement remains hidden.

- Now this leaves our young writers the task of devising up to six clues that will point in the direction of the solution. Once the clues have been agreed they should be typed into the surrounding boxes. This makes for a good guided task with a group of up to six children. Click 'Reveal' to uncover the solution to the mystery.

- Finally, ask the children to use copies of photocopiable page 32 to help them independently devise a mystery and to think of clues that will be pieced together to solve it. Explain it is important that when these clues are placed in a story, they are spread throughout the narrative and found one by one. Putting the clues together to solve the mystery should be a challenge for both the reader and character in the story.

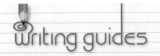

Activity 9: The 'It' factor

Objective

To select and use a range of technical and descriptive vocabulary (Year 3 Strand 9).

What's on the CD-ROM

Media resources
● Use the image of the 'Ghoul' as a stimulus for writing.

What to do

This activity gets children devising their own 'It'.

● Display the image of the 'Ghoul' from the 'Media resources' section of the CD-ROM. Explain to the children that many scary stories feature an 'It', the scary thing that lurks out there – whether it be a ghoul, like this one, a giant shark or a vampire.

● Ask the children to list, verbally, other various nasty and scary creatures that inhabit the stories they have encountered. Point out that these can take many forms but tend to be evil characters, monsters or ghouls that inhabit regions in the story and are to be feared.

● Invite the class to work in pairs, and hand out copies of photocopiable page 33. Read out the 20 planning questions which should help them devise an 'It'. Tell them to begin by selecting and cutting out the ten questions they think are the most important for devising a good 'It'. Then work through the ten questions, making notes around them and answering each one.

● Using their notes, tell them to plan and write a story about their 'It'.

Activity 10: Character file

Objective

To use setting and characterisation to engage readers' interest (Year 4 Strand 9).

What's on the CD-ROM

Character file
● Create a villain (shady character) by typing in relevant details about them.
● Select and drag an image of a villain into the character profile.

What to do

Using the character file the children can devise villains with features that will make them interesting characters for a scary story.

● Open the CD-ROM file 'Character file' (or use photocopiable page 34 'Character file') and name the villain and his crime. Ask the children to select and drag a 'mugshot' from the 'Image bank' to use for their villain. The children will then need to write a description. They could focus on what makes their character scary.

● The section marked 'How to investigate them' requires the children to work backwards: from the villain and his or her crime, the children have to decide how the wrongdoing will be uncovered. They might want to refer to their work on clues and suspense.

● Point out to the children that when they move on to think of a secret for a character, they are devising something that will need to be revealed later on in the story. This is a vital aspect of story planning in the scary story or mystery genre. Children will often plan the opening of a story and then slam straight into the closure of their tale. Planning a course of events that will confound the villain encourages a more gradual and organised process of deciding what the villain's secret is and how it will gradually be uncovered.

● The CD-ROM enables the children to save their character file. Allow the children the opportunity to select and incorporate their own villain and those created by other children into their own scary story.

Are you getting scared?

● Write five fears in the empty boxes and then surround each of them with descriptive words or reasons for this fear.

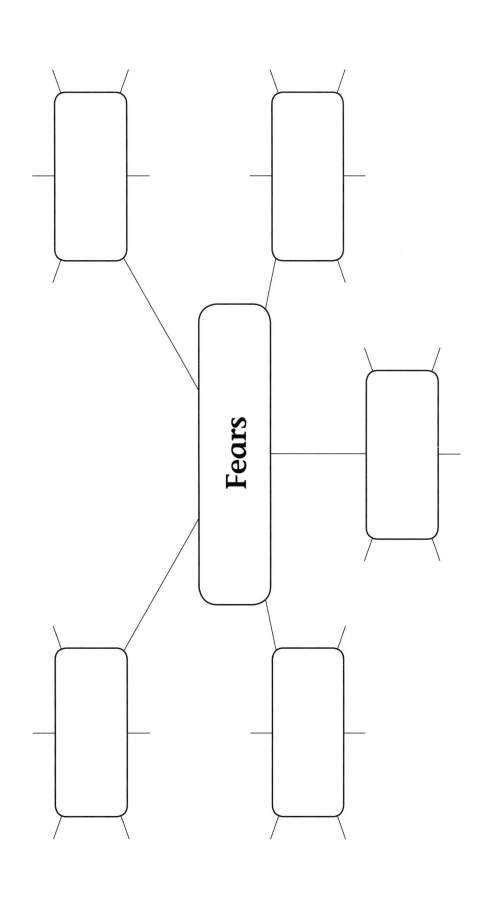

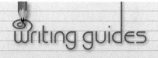

Feature feelings

● As a character moves through a scary setting, he or she will think and feel different things.

● What might your character think and feel when seeing…

Illustrations © 2001, Sarah Warburton.

Feature feelings paragraph

● Select the mysterious feature you find most interesting from 'Feature feelings' (locked door, prowler, trapdoor or hidden key). Then plan and write a paragraph for a story which begins with a character seeing your chosen feature.

Feature

Questions

Hunches

Feelings

Just then I saw a.....

Illustrations © 2001, Sarah Warburton.

Photocopiable ■SCHOLASTIC
www.scholastic.co.uk

Scary places!

● Different features make a setting scary. Plan your own scary setting by selecting and describing certain features. Then bring these features together to write a descriptive paragraph about your scary setting.

Time of day

Sounds

Descriptive paragraph

Location and its features

Weather

Illustrations © 2001, Sarah Warburton.

writing guides

Suspense planner

Imagine that a character is about to do something important, such as open a trapdoor. The writer can delay this moment but the reader wants to know what will happen. This is called SUSPENSE.

- Here is an example of how to delay a key event in a scary story.

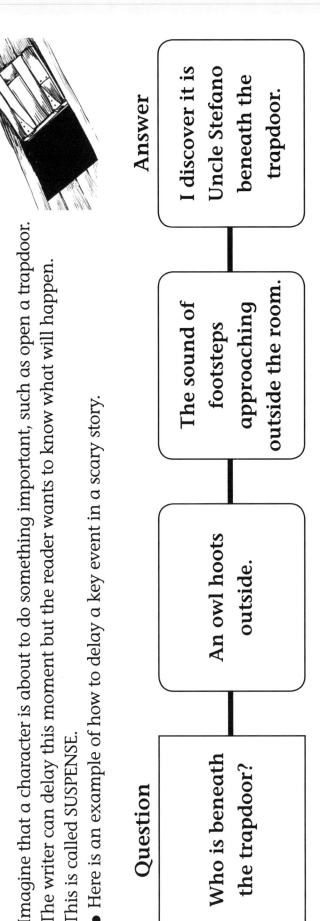

Question

Who is beneath the trapdoor?

An owl hoots outside.

The sound of footsteps approaching outside the room.

Answer

I discover it is Uncle Stefano beneath the trapdoor.

- Think of an important event to use in your own scary story and then two delays to keep your reader in suspense.

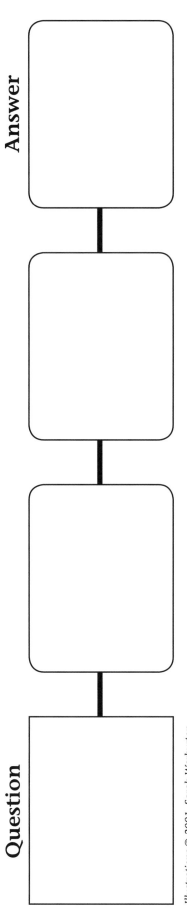

Question

Answer

Illustrations © 2001, Sarah Warburton.

Reading questions

• When things happen in mystery stories, readers ask questions. For example: when someone finds a key, the reader asks: "What will it open?"

• What could you put in your story that will cause readers to ask questions?

When...	my reader will ask... ?
When...	my reader will ask... ?
When...	my reader will ask... ?

How will your ending work?

Bin bag clues

● Can you solve the mystery? Here are some clues found in the bin of the character who has mysteriously vanished. Using five of these clues piece together the last things the character did before vanishing.

Illustrations © 2009, Sarah Warburton.

Photocopiable | 📖 **SCHOLASTIC** www.scholastic.co.uk

Clues

● Think of a mystery that your character could solve. What clues will your character find to solve the mystery? Complete the boxes below.

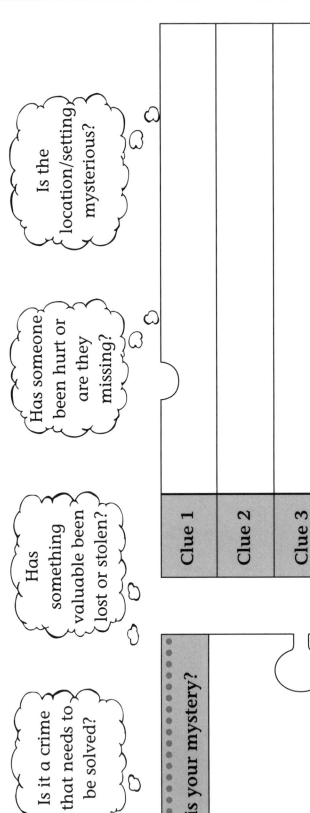

Is the location/setting mysterious?

Has someone been hurt or are they missing?

Has something valuable been lost or stolen?

Is it a crime that needs to be solved?

Clue 1	
Clue 2	
Clue 3	
Clue 4	
Clue 5	
Clue 6	

What is your mystery?

Illustrations © 2001, Sarah Warburton.

The 'It' factor

- In many stories there is a creature, ghoul or spook that scares the main characters. Use ten of these questions to come up with your own ideas for a story about 'It'.

What noises do we hear it making?	What does it do?	What it is like?	Where it is?
What do we think about it?	How does it start to scare us?	How do we end up near it?	What horrible thing does it do to make us really scared?
How does it finally catch up with us?	What happens when we hide from it?	Where do we run to escape from it?	What happens when we finally confront it?
How do we leave it?	How can we finally defeat it?	What does it want?	How did it get there?
			What it is?
			What clues does it leave to tell us it's around?
			What do we say when we discuss it?
			Where do we find out a way to defeat it?

Section 2: Developing writing

Character file

- Devise a character. Make them a villain, crook, shady type or probable suspect.

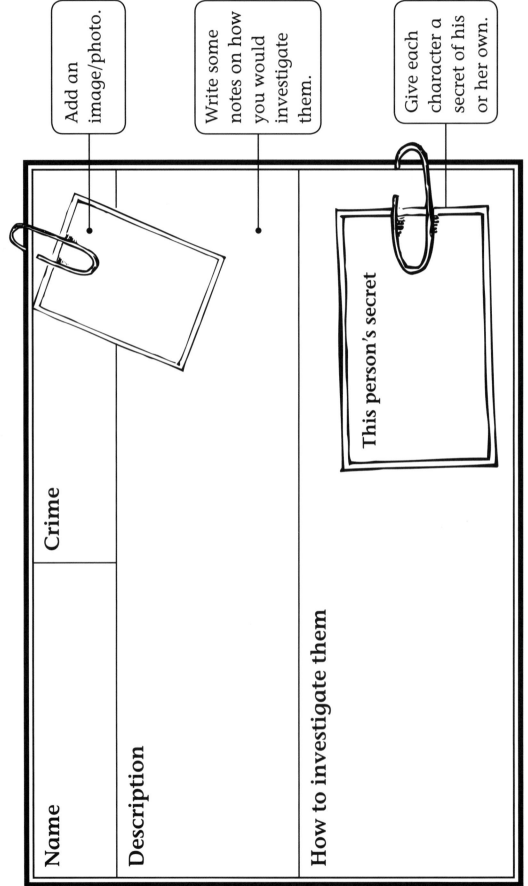

Name		Crime
Description		
How to investigate them		This person's secret

Add an image/photo.

Write some notes on how you would investigate them.

Give each character a secret of his or her own.

writing guides

Section 3

Writing

Having read some good examples of scary writing, taken some key ideas from these and had a play with them in Sections 1 and 2, children should be straining at the leash to write their own scary story. This section introduces three writing projects that can be used to resource guided writing and independent work. The three projects are all very different but each one is designed to aid the children in formulating ideas and ultimately creating effective scary stories.

'Our scary story' focuses the children's attention on the importance of planning before they begin to write a story. Through discussion and questioning ideas are stimulated for different aspects of a scary story including the characters, setting and plot. The children are then given the opportunity to choose, plan, develop and write a particular section of the story.

'Sensing suspense' centres on the idea that, in many scary stories, there is an 'It' creature, monster or ghoul that is lurking somewhere waiting to spring itself on our characters. It's seldom revealed quickly – think how long viewers wait for the shark in 'Jaws' to show its face. For much of the story the menace lies below the surface. The aim of this project is to encourage the children to carefully contemplate the build up to the scary encounter and to use their senses to help create a paragraph full of suspense.

'Gloom House' presents two specific photocopiable resources with scary features designed to stimulate the children's story writing. They introduce characters, objects and scary settings that can be used to stimulate thoughts around the mystery to be solved and the questions the reader will ask. Through this project the children will come to appreciate that time taken over creating a character's profile and the scary setting will pay off in the resultant story.

Using the writing templates

The 'My scary story' file on the CD-ROM allows children to produce their own scary stories by combining images and text. The writing frame provides various templates that can be used in two ways – the children can type their stories directly into the writing templates and then save and print out their work. Alternatively the blank layouts can be printed out to be filled in by hand.

There is a wide selection of images available in the 'Image bank' that the children can insert into the writing templates to illustrate their scary story. It is also possible for them to upload their own images, including hand drawn images of scary characters, settings and scenes, into the 'Our images' section of the 'Image bank' (see 'Help file' on the CD-ROM). Once the scary story is complete click on 'My cover' and let the children design a cover for their story.

Writing tips

When writing a scary story:
- Create typical scary characters, settings and events.
- Develop characters by describing what they do, say, think and feel.
- Use adjectives, adverbs, powerful verbs, similes and metaphors to describe people, places, objects and events.
- Use connectives to link events, build suspense and shift attention.
- Include questions to involve the reader.
- Use 'story ingredients': opening, build-up, challenge, events, resolution and ending.

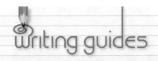

Project 1: Our scary story

Objective

To use beginning, middle and end to write narratives in which events are sequenced logically and conflicts resolved (Year 3 Strand 9).

What's on the CD-ROM

Blue group's story plan
- Pose and type in questions and ideas.
- Roll over text to reveal further ideas.

Scary plan
- Complete the story planning frame.

My scary story
- Compose a story using the writing templates.

What to do:

This project focuses the children's attention on the important task of planning, before they begin to write a story.

- Open the CD-ROM file 'Blue group's story plan' and ask the children to imagine they are members of the blue group and read through the basic story plan. After reading the initial plan, ask if they can think of any questions or points to add to the ideas shown and type them in.

- Discuss their ideas and then roll over the initial plan created by the blue group to reveal a collection of stimulating questions and ideas, which can help bring out the best in the planned story. This model aims to emphasise how planning can enrich a story and involves the children in offering their own thoughts. Did the children suggest the same ideas? What other ideas did they have?

- Now ask the children to take the idea of Fang Castle and try writing a particular section of the story – such as Carys persuading Karl to get the ball. Once they have made their selection, open the 'Scary plan' in the 'Planning' section of the CD-ROM and give them time to make further notes and develop their selected section of the story.

- Open the 'My scary story' writing frame and ask the children to select a blank layout on which to begin writing. Demonstrate how to add text and insert and resize images from the 'Image bank' (see Help file).

- The children may also use the blue group's model story plan as a stimulus to explore questions they can use to enrich their own stories.

Project 2: Sensing suspense

Objective

To show imagination through the language used to create atmosphere and suspense (Year 4 Strand 9).

What's on the CD-ROM

Sensing suspense
- Type notes about a character's senses.
- Type a suspense-filled paragraph.

My scary story
- Compose a chapter using the writing templates.

What to do

This project concentrates on developing the children's ability to create suspense moments, which are so crucial in scary stories.

- Start the lesson by explaining to the children that what we tend to remember from watching scary films, are the steps towards a scary encounter, rather than the actual encounter itself.

- Open the CD-ROM file 'Sensing suspense', which aims to develop the children's writing in the direction of one crucially scary paragraph. It focuses on building up the sentences that describe a character's steps towards whatever it is they will encounter. As a class discuss and make notes on how a character's senses can be utilised in order to create suspense and atmosphere in a scene.

- The activity in the CD-ROM file and photocopiable page 39 draws on the senses and can be done as a drama activity, with the children imagining each step and making their notes.

- When the children have drafted their suspense-filled paragraph, open the CD-ROM file 'My scary story', select a blank layout and then ask them to develop their paragraph further, perhaps into a chapter.

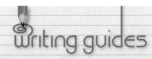

Project 3: Gloom House

Objective

To use setting and characterisation to engage readers' interest (Year 4 Strand 9).

What's on the CD-ROM

Gloom House
- Select a location on the map and roll over it to reveal questions to answer about how it could form a scary setting.

Wild cards
- Select cards containing features that will form the basis of a scary story.

Scary plan
- Complete the story planning frame.

My scary story
- Compose a story using the writing templates.

What to do

For this project the children select key elements to incorporate into a scary story.

- Open the CD-ROM file 'Gloom House'. This map provides a starting point and questions to prompt thoughts about a story setting. Ask the children to select a location from the map, think about how it may feature in a story, then call up, discuss and answer the questions.

- Hand out copies of photocopiable page 40 'Gloom House' and encourage small groups of children to plan a route through the map. Ask: *Why would someone go there? Could they be there by accident? Who or what would they encounter? Where would they end up?* As they suggest ideas, invite them to write on their own copy of the map. Gradually, the step-by-step development of a story will emerge.

- Different groups can work on developing ideas for selected settings and address the CD-ROM questions. They should think of descriptive words to draw the atmosphere around their account of this setting.

- Next, open the CD-ROM file 'Wild cards' (or use photocopiable page 41) and click on one card from each category (character, setting and object). Then as a class use the features on the three selected cards and build up ideas around them which will form key elements to a scary story. After linking these features together to make a story, the children can add other characters, settings or objects as they wish.

- Ultimately, this can lead to the children writing a story involving all the wild cards and their own features. However, it is worth bearing in mind some aspects of writing that are particularly supported by these cards:
  - Character cards encourage thought about the personality they inject into their story, rather than just writing about some flat characters.
  - Setting cards encourage movement around an imaginary region.
  - Objects raise questions that can suggest a whole narrative, such as: Why is there a piece of paper inside the bottle?

- Using two character cards, a pair of children could devise a conversation. They could say the dialogue aloud, reworking it as they develop a scene.

- This material is open-ended. The children could devise new wild cards, imagine what lies beyond the edges of the map, plan the inside of Gloom House, or invent a system of tunnels connecting a few locations.

- When the children have a collection of ideas they need to bring them together and form a plan for a story using the 'Scary plan', which is on photocopiable pages 42–43 or in the 'Planning' section of the CD-ROM.

- When their plans are complete open the CD-ROM file 'My scary story' and select a blank layout to open a page. Explain that this is going to be the first page in their story. Demonstrate how to add text and insert and resize images from the 'Image bank' (see Help file). Once the children understand how the writing templates work allow them to start writing their own scary story.

Blue group's story plan

Setting

Village of Fang Castle

Plot

Karl loses ball in Fang castle.

Carys persaudes Karl to go and get it

They go to get it

Dr Fang imprisons them

Carys tricks Dr Fang and escapes

Karl escapes

Frees the other children

They find the monster

They all get away and Monster is their friend

Secret

Castle Bolivang contains a monster, invented by Doctor Fang

Characters

Doctor Fang – evil. Horrible to the children in the village

Bombo the Monster

Karl – nervous boy. Good at football.

Carys – bravest girl. Very confident.

writing guides

Sensing suspense

● Imagine your character is about to encounter something scary. Draw on your knowledge of the senses and make notes to help set the scene and build suspense.

What did the character see?

What did the character hear?

What did the character smell?

What did the character feel as they reached out?

What did the character think?

What did the character say out loud?

Illustrations © 2009, Sarah Warburton.

● Use your notes to write a suspense-filled paragraph.

Gloom House

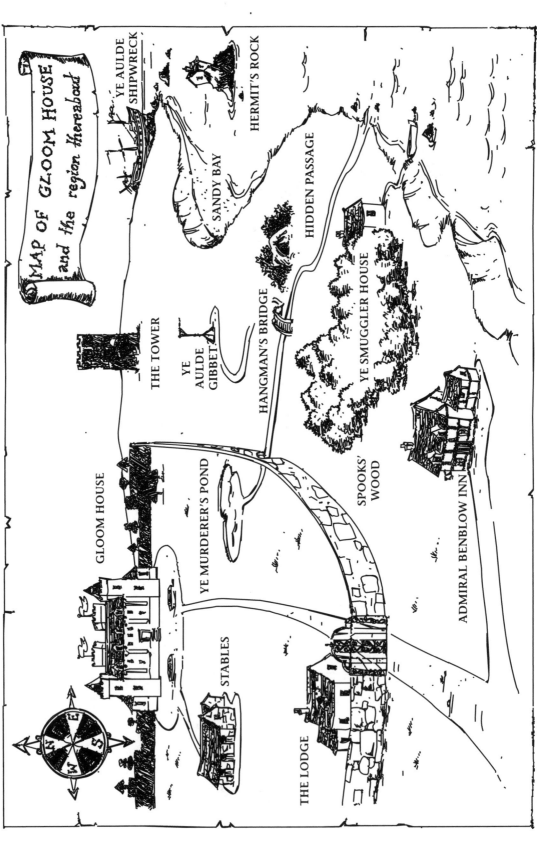

MAP OF GLOOM HOUSE and the region thereabout

YE AULDE SHIPWRECK

HERMIT'S ROCK

SANDY BAY

HIDDEN PASSAGE

THE TOWER

YE AULDE GIBBET

HANGMAN'S BRIDGE

YE SMUGGLER HOUSE

GLOOM HOUSE

YE MURDERER'S POND

SPOOKS' WOOD

ADMIRAL BENBLOW INN

STABLES

THE LODGE

Illustrations © 2001, Sarah Warburton.

Wild cards

● Use a selection of these cards to produce ideas for a scary story.

Scary plan

● Plan your scary story by making notes about the key elements it will involve.

Main character(s)	'It' creature(s)

Scary setting(s)	Mystery object(s)

Suspense moments

Questions raised

Resolution and ending

Section 4

Review

Ongoing formative assessment of children's learning in writing is essential. It allows teachers to evaluate the progress that children are making towards achieving specific learning targets and to plan the next steps in learning at an appropriate level. It is also important to make an overall review of children's progress at the end of a unit of work to review work against national standards and identify gaps in teaching and learning.

Self review

In order to involve children fully in their learning it is important that they are included as much as possible in the assessment process. Photocopiable page 45 is a self assessment tool designed to be used by the children working independently, to review how successful they have been in using some of the characteristic style/language features of the scary stories genre in their own writing. You may wish to model the self review process first, using one of the shared stories created by the whole class.

Peer review

Photocopiable page 46 encourages the use of writing partners to help children review and develop their written work. The children should work in groups of three, reading each other's stories and completing the 'story changing chart' for each story except their own. They should use the sheet to keep a tally of the review as it progresses. As a result, different perspectives will feed into the editing process. Having tried this with someone else's story, the children should be able to confidently apply this chart to their own writing. Redrafting from scratch can be tedious, but the understanding of how a story can be improved by reworking specific passages is a vital part of the writing process. Using a word processor will speed up the editing process. Remind the children that their comments to each other should be constructive and supportive.

Assessing children's progress - Teacher review

The grid on photocopiable page 47 has been designed to enable you to assess the children's progress and attainment in writing at the end of a scary stories unit of work. It is linked to the National Curriculum's eight assessment focuses for writing. When reviewing children's work in relation to each assessment focus, it is important to use a range of evidence, including observation (contributions made in speaking and listening and drama activities) as well as assessment of written work.

Carrying out such a review will enable you to evaluate the progress individual children have made towards achieving specific learning goals. The findings of the review should be used to set group and individual learning targets and to ensure that the next steps in learning for all children are planned at the appropriate level. The review may also highlight any gaps in teaching and learning. If this is the case, identify and address these gaps by revisiting the relevant lessons in Section 2.

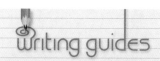

Self review

Read your story and use the grid below to record what features made your story scary.

My scary story is called...

_____

_____

_____

I used this sentence to begin my story

_____

_____

_____

Words I used to describe the scary setting

_____

_____

_____

Words or sentences I used to link events in my story

_____

_____

_____

An example of dialogue that creates suspense in my story is...

_____

_____

_____

My scary story is...

Not scary   **Extremely scary**

Illustrations © 2001, Sarah Warburton.

Photocopiable ■SCHOLASTIC www.scholastic.co.uk

Peer review

Story changing chart

_____'s story

something you would change about a character
two new words you would use to describe the setting
something else a character could have said
a different opening line
a different closing line

Attach this to the original story for the writer to use.

Story changing chart

_____'s story

something you would change about a character
two new words you would use to describe the setting
something else a character could have said
a different opening line
a different closing line

Attach this to the original story for the writer to use.

Illustrations © 2001, Sarah Warburton.

Teacher review

	AF5 Vary sentences for clarity, purpose and effect	AF6 Write with technical accuracy of syntax and punctuation in phrases, clauses and sentences.	AF3 Organise and present whole texts effectively, sequencing and structuring information, ideas and events	AF4 Construct paragraphs and use cohesion within and between paragraphs	AF1 Write imaginative interesting and thoughtful texts	AF2 Produce texts that are appropriate to the task, reader and purpose	AF7 Select appropriate and effective vocabulary
LEVEL 3	Consistent use of past tense throughout writing. Uses a mixture of simple and compound sentences, some complex sentences may be used with support.	Use of full stops, capital letters, exclamation marks and question marks to demarcate sentences is generally accurate. Some attempt to use speech marks to punctuate direct speech.	Writing shows evidence of attempt to organise ideas in a chronological sequence. Opening and endings usually clear.	Organises story content into simple paragraphs. Attempts to use connectives to signal time and place and give coherence to writing within paragraphs.	Content and ideas are appropriate to the task. Uses adjectives and adverbs to add interest for the reader.	Attempts to write in an appropriate style, demonstrating some awareness of reader (e.g. using different techniques to provoke reader reactions).	Uses a range of nouns, verbs, adjectives in writing to add interest for the reader.
LEVEL 4	Secure control of tenses in both narrative and dialogue. Some variation in sentence structure and length. Subordinating connectives (e.g. because) if used to create some complex sentences.	Accurate demarcation of sentences throughout the text. Direct speech mostly correctly punctuated with speech marks. Some accurate use of commas to mark clauses.	Clear openings and closings that are sometimes linked. Ideas mainly organised in a logical sequence.	Uses paragraphs to organise content. Uses some conjunctions and adverbs to establish links within and between paragraphs.	Content and ideas relevant to task. Some expansion in noun phrases and adverbials to develop scary characters and settings. Characterisation developed through description and dialogue.	Uses and adapts features of scary stories in own writing (e.g. building suspense, a back story). Purpose of writing is clear although may not be maintained throughout.	Some imaginative vocabulary choices used for effect (e.g. to create atmosphere, build suspense).

Also available in this series:

ISBN 978-1407-11253-4

ISBN 978-1407-11265-7

ISBN 978-1407-11267-1

ISBN 978-1407-11256-5

ISBN 978-1407-11270-1

ISBN 978-1407-11248-0

To find out more, call: **0845 603 9091**
or visit our website: **www.scholastic.co.uk**